T0146645

Heart of Faith

Anjali Kakar

authorHOUSE®

AuthorHouse™ UK
1663 Liberty Drive
Bloomington, IN 47403 USA
www.authorhouse.co.uk
Phone: 0800 047 8203 (Domestic TFN)
*   +44 1908 723714 (International)*

© 2016 Anjali Kakar. All rights reserved.

*No part of this book may be reproduced, stored in a retrieval system, or transmitted
by any means without the written permission of the author.*

Published by AuthorHouse 07/13/2016

ISBN: 978-1-5246-3701-9 (sc)
ISBN: 978-1-5246-3700-2 (e)

Print information available on the last page.

*Any people depicted in stock imagery provided by Thinkstock are models,
and such images are being used for illustrative purposes only.
Certain stock imagery © Thinkstock.*

This book is printed on acid-free paper.

*Because of the dynamic nature of the Internet, any web addresses or links contained in this book may have changed
since publication and may no longer be valid. The views expressed in this work are solely those of the author and do
not necessarily reflect the views of the publisher, and the publisher hereby disclaims any responsibility for them.*

Contents

Introduction

These poems revolve around the story of a girl whose ideas are vast and who wants to explore the world, fall in love, live like a leading character in a novel, and feel like a thousand bubbles are bursting inside her. Her passion for work is beyond our comprehension. While she projects an immensely strong image, she has always struggled inside. However, she is someone who diligently believes in her own faithful heart as she drives through life's dark alleys and narrow paths. She has come a long way in her life and now draws from an unlimited reservoir of potential. Her true purpose is to light lanterns in other people's lives.

Unity in Diversity

In 1985, the journey begins.
Vast ideas lead to the gigantically magnanimous birth of an airline.
Seemingly unknown, it remains desirably unaltered.
Rising of the sun, stepping ahead in the journey. Here begins its shine:
One man, one soul, with a vision larger than life,
Is also an innovator, profound thinker, philanthropist, and chairman.
Having mastered all aspects, he acquires the role,
Leasing the first aircraft.
It is a humongous work of fine craftsmanship. Ideas are presented
And implemented, but they are scattered on a raft.
He leads the company through a merger and hires people across the world.
Funny as it may sound,
Seems as if wrapped in a curl.
Quotes, advertisements, and the brand image leave you stunned.
He captures the entire universe. Discrimination? None.
He lives in isolation, being on the top.
Salute the chairman!
He is astoundingly ambitious, and his remarkable ideas frequently crop up:
He sponsors cricket, rugby, tennis, and football.
He mesmerizes hearts, but his curiosity prevails—is that all?
His fleet's interiors make his aircrafts breathtaking.
Immense hard work and brainstorming led to their making
Upon rock-solid foundations.
They were pieces of work a decade before the company's destination:
Unity in diversity, ecstatically intriguing,
And demographically diversified.
These are primarily the reasons the company is leading
The transformation of an airline to a brand
Across the globe with a million admirers.
The reason it's a brand is justifiable.
Years pass in the glimpse of an eye,
And its journey has been unfathomable:
Incorrigible and dauntless, it will never say goodbye.

Unity with Alien

Ladies and gentlemen, let me engage you
In a journey back about which I had no clue.
It's the story of a man
Whose curiosity prevails. He's trapped as if in a can
A million miles away,
Emitting light, a shining ray
Aimed at planet Earth.
With vast ideas, wrapped in blue robes,
This is about his journey, its worth.
Innumerable questions are on his face,
But it's safer to be without expectations in this race.
Unity in diversity is captured by
Drawing while baffled. A moment of truth, a moment of lies.
Words, languages never heard before,
Emerge from … Where was the core?
Several nationalities across the globe
Are embedded in different colors, as a prince would be
Wrapped in a diamond robe.
These cultures become one amalgamation.
Their beauty is captured in the sun's reflection.
Madonna to Michael Jackson rocks.
They rejoice with excitement, appearing on the block.

Alien: What brings this world together?

Narrator: It's the dance and music in our hearts
That rains forever (in video)
And sings and dances around the trees,
Unfolding the dramatic mysteries of life.
The European continent is the key.
Moves leave you stunned.
American culture has no discrimination,
Rolling with beats, snapshots of rum.

Africa is mesmerizing with its rhapsodic drums,
Merging the entire planet
In an expression of freedom, dancing beautifully
With crowned ornaments. Planet Earth is the king.

Alien: Wow! I am astounded by the beauty
Of people singing and dancing together and residing in unity.
Let me head back to where I belong.
Grateful for the moments captured, I am awakening
With the rising dawn.

Learning in Diversity

Learning and development are established entities.
Vast ideas and astounding talent are in scarcity.
Enhancing personality, polished knowledge and skills
Are gatekeepers of destiny, enriching those who have the will.
Training needs analysis to evaluation.
Primarily defined existence, contribution to organization
Factors, processes, products, pricing …
Significantly embracing people is the reason why L@D is rising.
Incorporating Gagné's models, or Kirkpatrick's across the globe,
Is one of innumerable strategies for implementing learning of this scope.
Comprising four quadrants, expanding horizons,
Training ghettos, learning leadership, comfortable extinctions, competitive risings,
Targeting nails on their heads, returns of investments that exceed the costs:
These are contributions toward business development. Forefront is L@D.
Overall, changes in personality are assets to the organization, as employees are the key.
Monitoring, measuring, recognizing, going all the way …
Moments are captured: laughter, presentations, and workshops with the dawn of shining rays.
Magnanimously giving and mesmerizing people comprise the core.
An insatiable and unfathomable unfolding has captured as far as, perhaps, a shell on the shore.

Love

Love is a feeling that comes to everyone.
It occurs between two persons, and the second one, who is unknown to you, becomes known to you in a fraction of a second.
Love makes you play, sing, dance,
Fly high up in the sky,
Twitter like birds, gutter like waterfalls.
It makes you feel incomprehensible; it even makes you cry.
Death lays her icy hands on you and makes you die
But never says goodbye!

My First Crush

Virtually rhapsodic at the age of sixteen,
I met my first crush, who was also a teen.
Seems my feelings were ecstatic in those days,
But I forget they were nothing but the beginning rays.
Whenever he came in front of me, nervousness made me run as if I were on a hunt.
Seldom I felt like listening to something.
Seldom I felt like saying something.
I didn't acquire guts and probably could do nothing.
Days seemed to be really short.
Nights seemed to be longer.
My eyes eagerly waited for him.
Soon my introduction to his girlfriend made me realize
He was nothing but melting ice.
Getting depressed, I finally realized
That life goes on and on, and crushes come and go,
But it's your first crush you will always remember from a long time ago.

Loneliness

Away from the world
Where no one resides
Stays loneliness
Within a hidden side.
No scream, no shout
Stays alone, free from doubt.
Occasional tears shed out of eyes
Make you aware of being connected to the universe.
It's scary, though, and threatening. Life seems rotten.
When you're surrounded by insecurity, nothing seems to have purity.
You feel the necessity of a partner.
Time seems to hold still.
Tears shed out of eyes
Seem to saturate as if this were the end of your life.
They seem to eat you up, disturbing both sides.
You need someone to fill the empty space,
To go on slow and steady in this unwrapped journey of life's race.

Two Lives Torn Apart

Two human lives suddenly torn apart
Bring a drastic change and an excruciating pain.
Commitments lie in the past.
Life passes by in the blink of an eye; it changes quite fast.
Days lie empty.
Nights you lie wondering.
But there's something that compels the eye to favor
Tears left in the eye.
No one even questions the reason why
It happens most of the time
That life, a burden for these two lives,
Forces them, due to circumstances, to lay their life together by the wayside.
Though life separates,
Death brings them together as they embark toward the heavenly gate.

First Love

Remembrance of first love captures you
Ecstatically. The world seems to be a better place.
Everyone's ignorance is no bother.
It's only love that remains.
Faith in the universe encourages.
It's the passage of time that disgraces.
Commitment on your side
Goes against enforcing people on the other side.
Wonderful nights seem to be forgotten.
In an instant life becomes virtually rotten.
It seems like the end of the world.
You perpetuate thoughts of the past, moments captured. You feel depressed.
The saying goes that everything happens for the best,
Helping unfold the uncaptured mysteries of life and leaving it for the rest.

So Close Yet So Far

So close yet so far,
The time taken should be measured in an hour.
Comparing knowledge is widespread.
It almost stretches like a thread.
Two people, so close yet so far,
Compelled by various reasons
Impossible to define,
Almost like flowing wine,
Are not necessarily involved.
Sure, there's something that revolves.
Trust and understanding prevail in relationships
Huge and scattered, almost like sunken ships.
Or they are like hidden treasure once the depth has been measured.
A lot of questions wait on the face.
It's safer to be without expectations in this race.
Go on. We will find a way
As beautiful as the shining ray.
With sayings left behind, so close yet so far,
This friendship will last forever—even until the end of that hour.

Only for You

It's only for you. Lay life by the side.
Leave the world behind.
Keep everything aside.
It's only for you that I reside.
Tears are shed
And blood flows ceaselessly.
I will be there for you
Until life shows a red signal that claims me.
It's only for you that I care,
Because you are rare, someone with whom I can share.
I will be there for you.
I swear by the moon and the stars
That I will be there for you until the end of that hour.

Trust

A betrayal of trust
Left tears in the eye.
I'm unaware of the reason why
It happened for the first time.
It's as if he committed a crime
Considered the most important in life.
It pinches profoundly, almost like a knife.
No commitment either.
No formal consent of will.
These ways and means to kill
Cause a conversation to be held
That, for sure, will melt.
No basis left behind to knelt.
He left a mar on the face.
Why did he do this?
Why leave me deserted in a row?
I learned something
Incomprehensible to define:
Recovering takes time.
Losing requires seconds.
Trust betrayed is left in the air,
Waiting to return, to inspire care.

Search

When I saw him for the first time,
I pondered him and wanted him to be mine.
Sayings led us forward.
Some called it a crime.
I pleaded the one above.
Shattering, I felt a few drops of love
That perpetuated for a while.
I wandered for a while.
I expected one wrapped in purple robes to be kind.
Eyes like the sunrise, he mesmerized.
Helplessness surrounded me.
It seems he astounded me.
I was impelled by various steps,
But timidity made me erect.
Innumerable question marks were revolving
Around me, and it seemed I was evolving.
Incessantly a picture on screen
Makes my heart ponder, happily and keenly,
How the one perpetuates the universe that is in his care.
His care is made into destiny.
The one who possesses the world's key,
Without a doubt, absorbed one for me.

Scary Though

Ghosts, though, exist.
It takes a fraction of a second for the heart to resist.
Drops of perspiration trickle from the forehead.
We come across them when we read
Novels by anonymous writers.
We realize on the first page
That we are being urged toward rage.
A pseudonymously named boy
Mentions his experience, though
It has been scattered almost in a row.
Inserting a needle in eye
Causes blood to flow profusely, impelling us to cry.
Darkness all around
Pondered a while
Pinches, dragging us for miles.
Excruciating enough,
Darkness really seems rough.
We become captured by weird hallucinations
And imposing allegations.
Forgetfulness takes time,
And we cannot claim that it is a crime.
Relaxation might overcome,
But it also might take time for some.
Protection from within
Will threaten us until the awakening dawn.

Special Friend

Someone is in my life.
The thought of him being away pinches almost like a knife.
Who is he?
Where does he come from? I don't care.
It only matters that he is one of the rare
Aspirations that fly high.
He has left me with few words to say.
He may or may not come this way.
I'm relying on imagination
Until it becomes merely a destination.

Audible Silence

Silence speaks for me.
It is irrelevant, though, like a thwack on the door that requires no key.
Incessant sound captures thoughts gathered together as if in a row
That leads me to step in a graveyard.
Absolute silence
Is captured by unknown noises that cause depression and aggression.
Feeling claustrophobic, I seem to be unknown,
While acoustical sound seems to be known.
Strange, isn't it? Human beings who do not exist within it
Experience it while going through the poem.
One might ask, what is the connection?
Life goes this route as if dragged by affection.
Silence seems to be
Louder than sound.
Acquaintance is clearer
Than silence, which speaks
To express the desire to live.
Silence says life is beautiful
And gifted by the one wrapped in purple robes.
Hold it. Embrace it.
Pointless moments of regret gather
when I'm lying in the icy hands of rope.

Rediscovering Myself

Immense hope is manifested in life.

Innumerable obstacles are encountered, and they are inexplicably as sharp as knives.

Human revolution has gone through

Transformative paths by which we've realized our mission.

Tears have tumbled out of our eyes,

But we have discovered paths toward success and opportunities to rise.

Buddha's wisdom and Buddha's courage offer protection from heavenly deities.

Dauntless, his lofty spirit has absolute conviction.

He opens up life, and his is not driven by fiction.

Soon I will experience unsurpassed achievement

As beautiful as the shining ray.

I am determined to achieve my dream.

My thoughts are ceaselessly flowing.

They are attractive and irresistible, like a cherry on the top of a sundae full of cream.

I experience meaningful accomplishment every day.

Having absolute faith, strong conviction, and *ichinen* to achieve is the only way.

Hope

Immense hope flows ceaselessly
Accumulating good fortune.
Life seems to be in rhythm and in tune.
Journey back, and life was a tarnished mirror.
Once it was polished, everything started opening,
And I started discovering
I was expanding to be as vast as the universe.
No longer a curse,
I started to engage in vigorous efforts every day.
A thousand bubbles burst inside,
Waiting to see the morning ray.
My dauntlessly lofty spirit lives by my mentor's teachings,
Moving ahead,
Harboring no doubts,
And believing in myself.
Moments of despair can turn your face red,
But I have clear vision in my eyes.
I'm eagerly waiting for the sun to rise.
Victory matters
During periods of struggle when moments aim to be scattered.
A winning attitude toward life
Can be as wide as an ocean and as sharp as a knife.

Gazing at the Moon

One fine afternoon
I heard the twittering of birds
And saw the guttering of waterfall.
Wrapped in a blue carpet,
I was scorching hot as the sun rose.
Soothing sounds of the waves
Felt like untapped rays from a cave.
Crashing waves resonated in my ears
As I felt the freedom of absolute freedom
Accompanied by tears of joy.
I pondered for a while
Vast ideas
And magnanimous dreams beyond human comprehension.
A thousand bubbles burst inside.
Ecstatic energy prevailed, awaiting the joyous ride.
Unambiguity surfaced,
And I attained the unsurpassed way,
Eradicating the deluded chasing.

Learning and Development

The journey began a year ago.
Flowing ceaselessly, it was a marathon.
Mesmerized, captured by the field.
Inquisitiveness means curiosity is on the yield.
Knowledge of wealth was bestowed upon me,
Unlocking various doors by providing the key.
Emerging from exceptional guidance,
I've been repaying debts of gratitude, exploring several shades.
My journey has been predicted, and I have a known destination.
I am without doubt and do not offer a shred of negotiation.
Several questions emerge on the surface.
Innumerable expectations run the passionate race
Incorporating various models, denying training.
Eagerness prevails to be a part of the innings
And to embrace the facts, gratefully merging the reality
With the director, the great almighty.
Seemingly impossible ones dream.
This is represented by the symbolic representation of a cake with cream
Or of taking the initial step rather than the staircase.
Being well guarded and not swayed by greed will result in winning the race.
Repaying debts of gratitude
Is the path to the radiant light,
Where we undergo humongous transformation and climb several heights.

Bodhisattvas

Ceremony in the air.
Purpose. Rhythm of life: heart with which we care.
Bodhisattvas emerge from the earth.
Life passes by a glimpse and karma is allocated individually, depending on worth.
Chosen ones are we,
Tapping into the unlimited potential, unlocking mysteries of life.
Chanting *Nam Myoho Renge Kyo* is the key.
Huge responsibility is on our heads
As we learn enormously and several tears are shed.
Carving our own ways,
We rise above and beyond like the glimpse of the shining ray.
Destiny has been chosen, an undesirable path
Of choices and commitment to those choices.
Repairing means our future shall not fall apart.
Bestowing insatiable benefits,
A huge fundamental change awaits.
Fighting alongside with our mentors,
With hearts aligned in unity,
We know victory awaits a breakthrough.
Several tremors
Leave us unperturbed. We are not swayed by the eight winds.
Buddhism is a reason.
The stating heart is the king
Abandoning the misery
Awakening each of us to our purpose.
We set our eyes to our missions.
As unbelievable as it may sound,
We are the ultimate creation.

Shadow over My Head

I am living with a shadow over my head
Wrapped in purple robes, mesmerizing clouds above my bed.
This perpetuation of the past.
My moment of insanity might be captured, hopefully, at last.
I want to find a way back into love
As beautiful as the guttering of a waterfall.
Seldom may this be tough.
I am graciously opening my heart
To someone who doesn't tear it apart.
I am stepping in a new direction
With tons of dedication
And hoping for an inspiration.
A thousand bubbles may burst inside.
Commitments and relationships have rules one has to abide by.
I am opening up to a new life.
I may encounter bumps or potholes hidden deep inside,
But I am emitting positive frequencies to the universe.
Absolute faith won't be a curse.
Clear vision in my eyes
Hopefully will turn out to be wise.
My expectations are larger.
Obstinate behavior won't melt like ice.
Lovable, adorable, a giver: these are words describing me.
He will encounter the rest when he opens the shelves.
Life can be full of surprises.
The winner of the game is the one who rises.
Hoping for a miracle, I'm feeling shy.
When I capture the moment forever, tears may tumble ceaselessly from my eye.

Scar

There is a gaping hole in my heart
Perpetuating the past and the moments when we drifted apart.
Reasoning and overanalyzing, my heart's desire is to be a part.
I journey back and seldom recall moments
When I was the leading character in a novel.
A thousand bubbles burst inside.
Irreplaceable, can't be objectified.
A steep slope awaits an adventurous ride.
Setbacks are rejections of endorsements of life
Like penetrating needles and wounding knives that cause excruciating pain.
It's the end of an era. I lack direction. We merged in vain.
Surrounded by protective forces,
I'm showered upon by immense hope.
Tapping the reservoir of potential,
I align my heart and master my mind, which is my methodology for coping.
I await winter turning to spring
And Prince Charming on his galloping white horse.
Inexplicably captured: the moment when he presents me with a ring.

Moments of Desperation

Moments of hesitation
Courageously stood by me.
A profound relationship bonded you and me.
I recall the journey back to when I encountered you those days.
I was amazed by your amusement
Shining like a beautiful ray.
Unforgettable memories, awakened conversations,
And immeasurably good fortune accumulated,
Leading my life in a direction
Clouded by fundamental darkness, filled with delusion.
Acted as a messenger on behalf of my mentor.
Gave life a vision.
Dedicating this poem
Is a symbol of love and of being kind
By an incredible disciple who works tirelessly
To fulfill a mentor's dream
That has been engraved with a keen desire.

Met This Guy

This guy was sweet as honey,
But my heart questioned why.
He seemed unbelievable,
And the factor of time seemed mean.
A thousand bubbles burst inside.
The moment was captured incessantly; it flowed like a ride.
I felt anxiety and curiosity to meet.
Patience is a virtue sowed as a seed
That leaves an ambiguous picture in the eyes.
I had expectations of a rising sunrise.
Fear prevailed, though,
Encountered in a row.
A betrayal of trust had happened before,
But taking this next chance was the way to go.
A long journey lay ahead of me,
But faith was the key.
Hurdles welcomed me home,
And I eventually took an unsurpassed journey all the way.

Grandpa

Compassionate, considerate, lovable, and adorable,
Grandpa was a man of few words
And a lovely husband.
The moment that separated us was indeed hard.
Death laid her icy hands on him,
This perpetuated the past,
And the situation seemed grim.
I was shattered and devastated
Upon hearing the news.
Pulling back together,
I remembered that death is inevitable.
Escapism is inevitable.
Life exists after death.
Huge expectations can be met.
Deep desire is somewhere hidden.
He reposed as a human,
But now the journey may begin
Toward indestructible happiness
And absolute peace
And deep *ichinen* in my heart.
His soul may rest in peace.
A new life will soon emerge,
Drawing forth immense hope and the realization that he will eventually merge.

Change the World

Change the world for me.
My eyes long to see a glance of love,
But excruciating pain wells within me.
Remembering the past's astounding days kills me.
I'm thirsty for direction.
A moment, a journey. All my creation
Is imprisoned within boundaries of hopelessness.
I've heard voices scream
Within a prison of mess,
Longing for the day
To change the world, when the sun will glitter its dazzling ray.

Finding Myself

With a question mark on the face,
I'm feeling abandoned in the long race.
Marriage is a conventional lifestyle
Of perplexing thoughts, whether for a lifetime or a trial.
I'm awakening to a clear vision.
Question: what do I really want?
Fears of loneliness and insecurity hover incessantly and haunt.
I want to let go of desperation,
Which is a painful monster.
Happiness knocks on the door with an invitation:
Love life, it says. Enjoy life every bit.
This change of philosophy won't quit.
I'm dreaming big, and a realization is taking place.
It's wrapped in a blue carpet, with open arms:
A feeling of fulfillment that captures me along this race
And welcomes me with open arms and grace.

Many Human Lives

Many human lives have been subjected to the icy hands of death.
Death, which is supposed to be their final destination, has met
Innocent people passing by
Who leave thoughts like shining rays.
This occurred on February 1,
Resulting in people red with blood.
It's impossible to define,
But it happened due to decompression
Turning over. It seemed like an impossible mission.
People were trapped in claustrophobic
Space. It was scary for people who seemed to be acrophobic.
It was incessantly happening in one.
All were ending up in none.
I was made aware
Of people running everywhere.
A lot of questions were on their faces.
They were left behind without expectations for this race.
Efforts were put in,
But death lays her icy hands down and wins.
Being the player requires struggling
To win the ball on the court.
The prior mode
Resulted in innumerable queries.
Answers about the crash vary.
I have feelings of helplessness just thinking of the moment.
Something was destroyed into pieces that was once secured as an ornament.
Looking forward with an open eye,
I see that rarely do people yell, "My, my!"
Various aspects of life
Pinch like a knife.
They're acceptable though hard to survive.

Perpetuation

Treat your mother with care
Unless she leaves a vacant chair.
That would make her among the rare
People with false expectations in the air.
All sayings are left by the side.
Only virtual thoughts capture the mind.
A fraction of a second has been destined
No matter what has been seen,
Impelled by circumstances,
The situation enhances,
Impelling us to rely
On old people screaming, "My, my!"
Is this life? It takes turns
And results in heart burns.
We head forward like shining rays.
Another turn of life
With unfolded arms may come in your way.

Dreams

Those are mine,
Away from the world,
Full of aspiration
And innovative imagination.
Sail in them.
Hail in them,
Feeling as you've never felt before
And pleading for more
Away from those who roar.
They can't be reality.
What happens in them doesn't happen everywhere.
Dreams are rarely taken as the face of reality.
For a while they even seem annoying.
Rest all the same,
As they are amazing.
Even if you're well versed in chasing
Them, always wait for them.
There's a reason they enlighten us as we face,
Slowly and steadily, the crowded race.

Telephone

The telephone bell rings.
Ecstatic to know whether it's my ring,
I run down the stairs,
Where screams a child
Who fails to understand that the call is rare.
I'm excited and nervous.
The thought of having a conversation
Seems like a mission.
Having talked it all over for a short while,
We've got to go a long mile.
I'm leaving it to destiny.
Everything happens for the best,
So I'll claim it for the rest.

Thought of a Wonderful Day

Being there, happy and gay,
Your presence makes me realize
My identity, thereby virtualizing
Every morning' sunrise.
I see your face in his eyes.
I'm sitting by the waterfall, thereby
Guttering the sounds I hear
And perpetuating voices I have captured by
Missing the touch that felt
Me and the hands that held
Me. These sounds acquire the quality of thunder when snow melts.
Innumerable words define
These thoughts that are mine.
The fulfillment of contentment
Is considered by only a few to be an element.
Whatever may be will be.
Acquiring pleasure,
Though, is defined in terms of measure.

Fun Time

It's a fun time.
In the view of a few, it's a crime.
There's no botheration.
Surrounded by aspirations,
Flying high in the air,
I can say there's no one for whom I care.
We had memorable days
And great fun.
Dad was unaware,
And I felt like a free bird.
I could be heard,
But that quickly passed away.
Life will remain forever like the dazzling ray.

Unbreak My Heart

My heart was connected; a thousand bubbles burst inside.
Little did I know joyous moments would take me on a ride
Incessantly flowing like a waterfall, technology driven. It's the call.
Little did I know that endless shovels
On the platform would be capturing lies
And unlocking mysteries. The truth was revealed,
Penetrating through the universe. I've prayed a prayer that heals
From betrayals of trust, anxiety, loneliness, and surfaced emotions.
Love was bestowed extravagantly, which raises several questions
About forgiveness, compassion, and guidance as needed.
Emerging bodhisattvas of the earth, every ounce, every moment embraced
Brings suffering and excruciating pain.
My situation included 180-degree transformation. A dragon was king.
Complete surrender, embracing the new.
Awakening of the dawn, showering upon a queue.
Bring forth the reservoir of potential, and turn winter to spring.
Abandon isolation, and forget "what if?" Embrace what will be.
When unlocking the gigantic door of the universe, being determined is the key.

Journey Home

Ecstatic and enthusiastic, I feel rapture,
A moment that is purely captured.
This 180-degree transformation
Causes oneness of life and environment, unlike saturation.
Journey back to a huge disaster.
One might have to master feeling fated for elimination.
Hovering like a helicopter, moving past that which hinders,
When one masters one's mind, one captures the goodness.
Abandon dwelling on the past, which is merely a mess.
Embracing the feeling of forgiveness and limitless compassion
Is compulsory for self-healing.
Be determined to win the race
Without any assumptions, and have a compassionate trace.
As deep or hollow as it may sound,
Winning over one's fundamental darkness means wearing the priceless crown.
Journey back to change poison into medicine.
Be incessantly driven. It's magnetically proven
That surrendering to the universe and acquiring rapture is heaven.

Many in Body But One in Mind

Many in body but one in mind,
We journey together. Symbolic representation seems to be mine.
Trust, compassion, and a foundation built
Prevent isolating space or a platform of guilt.
Vast ideas
Bring forth opportunities for intervention
And for working together in collaboration.
Many in body but one in mind,
We are awakening to our mission.
Vast ideas enable the kind of creation
Taught by Nichiren Daishonin.
We are as inseparable as fish and water.
Daimaku leads to victories
That are indisputably on the rim.
The alignment of the mentor and disciple relationship
Creates causes for boarding the good-fortune ship.
Achieving *kosen-rufu*, the great vow,
Means eliminating practical efforts.
We must find unity in diversity. The question raised is, how?
To briefly summarize,
We are many in body but one in mind.
We have laid a unified foundation together that is dependent upon principles of being kind.

Raising a Child

Raising,educating children at home
Capturing Sensei's guidance, unfolding concealed mysterious from chrome.
Faith manifests itself daily life
Parents guarded, breathe, sitting on the edge of knife
Gongyo, diamaku imperative as it may be
Ignoring studies, fooling around, definitely not the key
Broadminded Parents, Engraving flexibility
Building a strong foundation, earning credibility
Brief encounter with your child
A warm hug that goes that extra mile
Purpose of our faith is to become wise
Getting bogged down on miniscule matters, feeling of being trapped, cage of mice
Responsible, considerate parents on the surface
Lacking heart to heart dialogue, living in a case
Important Hearts connected, where families merge together
Physical presence though, estranged from one another
Children keen perceptive than adults
Saddened when parents fight
Parents caution, thought, word, deed imp, making every moment right
Refrain from scolding children the same time
Perception of a child, nervous, rebellious, pondering, indulge in a crime
Immense affection, shower them with love
Life is unpredictable, oblivious to its curve
Be fair and don't compare
Bestowed upon with beautiful children, a gift to cherish is rare
Devoted, dedicated, parents of faith
Welcome your child, with open arms, inspissating strong bonds, opening the gate.

Depth of Emotion

A moment that captures, a moment that resides.
Unfolding mysteries capture the glimpse of an early sunrise.
Feeling like the leading character in a novel, I sense a thousand bubbles bursting inside.
Wrapped in purple robes, I'm in the moment, where the heart resides.
You make me smile and go that extra mile.
This journey is ceaseless like a waterfall. Perhaps it is my own creation.
I'm claiming to teach the world's facts
With glitter in my eyes. Should I react?
Astoundingly beautiful thoughts have so far been seen.
Curiosity prevails, so we seem a bit keen.
Hopefully life unfolds like a mesmerizing dawn
That's as beautiful as can be, like a prince drawing forth his diamond crown.

About the Author

Anjali Kakar is an extremely optimistic person and believes in fairy tales. Never giving up attitude has always been her strength. While she continues to draw forth her potential, these poems act as an instrument to her greater growth. Inspiring every soul and getting a smile on someone's face indeed makes her quite happy. While she incessantly explores and discovers the world, her passion for writing poetry has increased magnanimously.

Printed in the United States
By Bookmasters